J.F. FERRER

Planning the Small Wedding

Ideas & Guidance for Planning a Small & Fabulous Wedding

First edition

This book was professionally typeset on Reedsy.
Find out more at reedsy.com

Contents

Preface

Congratulations! This time in your life should be one of the happiest times. The last thing you would want is to diminish that happiness with a ton of stress while planning your wedding. I hope this book helps while planning your special day. This book is a guide written for a small wedding. It is a basic outline with advice and guidance on what to expect and plan for. This book is not a step-by-step book. It does not include every single detail of planning a wedding. If it did, this book would be never-ending. Instead, this book provides tips, ideas, and advice that I hope will help you in your wedding planning so you can have a memorable day for yourselves and all your guests.

Please keep in mind that your wedding day is YOUR SPECIAL DAY and that YOU are sharing this day and also planning this day with the person you love. Therefore, you two should have your wedding exactly how you want it, no matter what anyone says or thinks. This day is the chance to show your love for each other. You can make your wedding day the most memorable and meaningful day of your life.

1

Chapter 1 - Introduction

S o what is a small wedding? A small wedding or micro-wedding is a wedding with 50 people or less. As a former wedding planner who has worked in over 500 weddings and events throughout my career, I can attest that my small weddings were just as beautiful as my elaborate weddings with 100 people or more. If you are having a small wedding, be proud knowing that you are making the right decision and that it will be a fabulous event for all who attend.

Budget

Determining your budget is essential and should be discussed before contracts are signed and before any high-priced items are purchased. Your budget will help determine the number of guests you wish to have at your wedding reception or may even dictate the style of wedding you should have. Most ceremony venues charge a flat rate for their services. Most reception venues such as hotel banquet rooms or wedding halls will also charge a flat rate or price-per person. The good news is your small wedding has an opportunity to save money and can also make your wedding day more personalized and unique.

I once had a couple who chose a beautiful park by a river to have a stand-up ceremony with 15-20 of their closest friends and family. After this, they all boarded a private yacht. They celebrated onboard with a plated dinner, DJ, dancing, and a cruise on the river. What a unique and special beginning for their marriage.

Wedding Ideas & Favorites

A few of you have daydreamed about your wedding - imagined where you would have it, who would be at the wedding, and what you would be wearing. Now that the time to plan is finally here, it is essential to keep an open mind and look at ALL of your options. There may be wedding-type stuff you have never even thought of before. A great place to start is in front of your laptop online. Many brides utilize websites and apps to help them plan their wedding. Zola, The Knot, Wedding Wire, and Pinterest are just a few popular ones. The deluge of wedding info from these sights can make any person quite dizzy. The trick is to use only information that you want and need. The wedding planning process can be fun. Google can be your best friend during this time. In the google search bar, you can find information such as pricing on all things wedding related, where to find a wedding officiant, hotels and travel information, and so much more. In my opinion, the easiest way to stay focused is to have a handy dandy Wedding notebook or wedding planner that you can write in so that you do not forget all that you want for your wedding. There are many free and for-sale "wedding checklists" online that you can download and print out. Choose whichever one is the easiest for you to use. I am a big fan of the bride or groom who uses a simple notebook and 3-ring binder with pockets for all the collateral and brochures collected throughout their wedding planning journey. It's an easy and low-cost way to stay organized with your ideas and favorites.

2

Chapter 2 - Guest Count

When wedding professionals speak with you about the total guest count, that count includes you, your partner, the wedding party, and all your guests. Coming up with your guest count should be easy for a small wedding. Talk with your partner. Agree on who will be invited and stay within the number of guests agreed on. Let's avoid a battle or an increase in your guest count. Remember that deciding to have a small wedding has a few advantages.

1 - You will be with your closest friends and closest members of your family at your wedding. Fewer people means more time with them.

2 - The wedding experience can be of better quality because you are catering to a small group of people. Service, food & beverage, decor, photographs, etc. are usually better with a smaller group of guests than with a larger group of guests.

3 - I have learned in my several years of coordinating weddings that the fewer people at the wedding, the less chance of drama happening during your wedding. So, don't worry about shortening that guest list.

My advice is to schedule a time when you and your partner can sit down together and come up with your list together. Write down a list of names of your guests. Discuss and decide how many guests you think will RSVP and attend. Once the hour is up, take a break if you have not finished finalizing the guest list. Otherwise, this task can be frustrating. Come back to this task when you two are ready to finish writing your guest list.

Helpful Tip - *Do not feel obligated to invite anyone from the office, even if your co-worker or boss is someone you see every day. You are having a small & intimate wedding with only close family and friends. If your work buddy is truly a friend, they will understand and probably be secretly happy that they do not have to purchase a wedding gift or give up a weekend day to attend another wedding.*

Who is Paying for The Wedding?

In this day and age, most couples pay for their wedding. If you are lucky enough to have a parent or someone close to you help you with the cost, be a savvy shopper and help them spend their money wisely. Many couples will go over budget for their wedding. It happens. The best thing you can do is be realistic about what you want and stick to your estimated budget as close as possible. If you two are paying for your wedding, look at your finances and determine who can pay for what. If family members are contributing, be straightforward with them and communicate the prices and costs of the services/products. Many people do not know the cost of things needed for a wedding. Family members might have sticker shock when pricing wedding venues or flower arrangements. You might learn that a loved one can't help pay for the wedding. Have a backup plan. Obtaining a bank loan or no-interest rate credit card could help. In any case, remembering to be grateful and kind can go a long way. Manipulation or drama caused by you or a family member can ruin the fun of planning your dream wedding.

Helpful Tip - *Bring loved ones who are helping you pay for the wedding while you visit venues. I've taken couples with their parents on site tours of wedding venues. More often than not, the parents happily paid for the entire wedding.*

3

Chapter 3 - Colors & Themes

Colors

In the past, I have been able to help couples choose their colors. Believe me when I tell you that choosing colors is not just a woman's choice. Many men I have worked with have strong opinions about the theme or colors for their wedding. I once had a couple who loved football and the Denver Broncos even more. They decided to have a football theme wedding with a wedding cake in the shape of a football. Navy and orange linen draped the tables with navy and orange flower centerpieces. It was one of the most memorable and fun weddings I have ever had the pleasure of coordinating. A great way to help you and your partner choose wedding colors is to look through a wedding magazine. Focus on colors in the magazine. With scissors, cut out colors you both like. Once you have come up with samples of colors you both love, compare the colors and select 2-3 colors that go well together. If you can't decide, seek the help of a wedding professional such as a florist or a wedding coordinator. Even if the wedding professional shakes their head no to the colors you have chosen, remember this is YOUR wedding. So if you two love pink and purple polka dots with yellow and black stripes, then have pink and purple polka dots with yellow and black stripes everywhere. Just be sure you LOVE IT.

Themes

Once in a while, I would come across wedding clients that were eccentric, unique, quirky even. I love these types of couples as they tend to have stylized or themed weddings that break the rules of the typical traditional wedding. A good-themed wedding should be a reflection of the couple's personality. If you want a theme for your wedding, ask yourself if you wish to have a casual, semi-formal, or formal wedding event. Also, your wedding decor, invitations, wedding attire, and choice of venue should reflect the theme and style of your wedding.

Here are a few examples of popular themes:

- Beach
- Nautical
- Christmas
- Spring
- Bohemian
- Country
- Indian
- Persian
- Asian
- Star Trek
- Star Wars
- Dinosaurs
- Disney

The list is endless. If you do not want a theme or haven't defined one for your wedding, please know that this is fine. Focus on your wedding colors instead.

4

Chapter 4 - Venues

Selecting a wedding venue can be one of the most fulfilling tasks in the wedding planning process. However, if you haven't done your homework, It can also be a not-so-fun experience. Many wedding venues offer both the ceremony space and a reception space so that the wedding experience is efficient and fluid. You and your guests will not have to hop in a car and drive to two different places. A venue like this may have all the answers you want. Many of these venues offer several options in their wedding packages. These packages can already include many things you still need to check off your list. Food & beverage, table linens, DJ, and dance floor, may already be included. Some even include valet parking for your guests. But before you get excited, it is best to call these venues ahead of time and ask about their minimum guest count requirements for weddings, a general price for the number of expected guests, and the availability. Have that phone call with the venue to avoid wasting time. Visit only the places that fit your budget or that have availability. Call and speak to a wedding professional from that wedding venue first and do a bit of homework online researching their reviews before setting the appointment to visit.

Here are some questions to ask when searching for a wedding venue:

- What is the cost?
- What is included in the ceremony and reception?
- What availability do you have? Do you have weddings on the weekdays? (Choosing a weekday may discount the cost.)
- What are your minimum and maximum capacity?
- Do you perform wedding ceremonies here as well? What is included in that package?
- Are there options for having an indoor wedding versus an outdoor wedding? What if it rains?
- Where do guests park?
- What is close by? (i.e. accommodations, restaurants, tourist spots)
- Which vendors do you work with? Can I use my vendors?
- Is there a dance floor/ dance area?
- How about accessibility? Are stairs or doorways an issue for guests?

Ceremony Venues

Did you know small weddings have more options and flexibility than large weddings for their ceremony space? You can even choose to have some or all guests standing. Don't be afraid to think outside the box on this one.

Here are some ideas for ceremony spaces:

- A small countryside church
- A barn
- The backyard of someone's home
- On a beach during sunset or sunrise
- A movie theater
- At a library

- By the water near or on a dock
- At a park or campground
- In a garden
- On the steps of a museum
- Inside a museum
- In an outdoor patio overlooking a city skyline
- On a yacht
- On a cruise ship
- In an airplane hangar
- Poolside
- On a rooftop

A Short & Sweet wedding ceremony is the way to go and a blessing for everyone at your wedding. A short 15 - 25 minute long wedding ceremony is enough time for the couple to exchange vows and share this most memorable moment with their loved ones. Most adults have a tough time focusing on anything longer than 20 minutes and think of the children (if there are any) having to stay still and quiet for that long. The good news is that most wedding professionals will guide you and recommend a short ceremony versus a long-winded drawn-out ceremony. Please listen to them as they are the experts.

When searching for a wedding officiant, ask for recommendations from the wedding professionals you meet. They usually have a favorite person they enjoy working with and knows does a great job. I advise you to choose an experienced professional. Choose an officiant that you like, one who speaks well and that you will not mind being in all your wedding ceremony photos. It also helps to read their client reviews. You will know in your gut if you have chosen and hired the right person.

Reception Venues

Reception venues come in all styles, shapes, and sizes. Small weddings can be cost-saving compared to larger weddings. Also, food and beverage menus for the smaller wedding can usually be more flexible and have more options. Here are some ideas on wedding reception options:

- Sunday Brunch in a Park
- Picnic on a Beach
- A plated dinner in a private dining room of a restaurant
- A Hotel Banquet Room
- A patio reception
- A reception under a white tent
- A cocktail reception at someone's home
- A beach house or Airbnb
- A Meeting or Party Room at the Community Center
- A Country Club
- In a small private restaurant rented for only your event
- At a castle
- A dinner cruise ship
- A racquet & tennis club
- An estate, chalet, mansion, or lodge

And of course, all of these reception venues above can also be a place where you can hold the wedding reception.

Helpful Tip - *Look for wedding venues that are "All-inclusive." Wedding venues that can accommodate both the ceremony and reception at the same place are the best venues for a small wedding as they include almost everything you need and want for your wedding that day. Some venues even provide one of their wedding coordinators to assist you at the venue during your wedding.*

5

Chapter 5 - Invitations

Save the Date cards are cards that announce your wedding date to your wedding guests. Plans for your wedding may not yet be solidified or even started, but you should have a date in mind and your chosen venue reserved. Save the Date cards should be sent out 7-9 months before your wedding date. If you plan to have a destination wedding, Save the Date cards should be sent to your guests one year in advance. Sending the Save the Date cards a year in advance allows your family members and friends to save money and make room on their calendars so they can attend your wedding.

Should small weddings even send out Save the Date cards? That is entirely up to you. If you scheduled your wedding within six months of your wedding date, then there is no need to send out a Save the Date to your guests. You can send your invitations out instead.

Invitations may play a small role in your wedding planning compared to the other items you are preparing for, but invitations are important because first impressions are everything. An invitation should set the tone for the wedding and complement the feel and theme of your wedding. For example, one of my friends had a destination wedding in the Caribbean. Her Wedding Invitations had a beach theme with Caribbean colors. The style of their invitation was perfect and matched her theme. Your guest should see the invitation as a gift, a reflection of you and your mate's personality, and a theme reflected in the style of stationery you send to them. If done correctly, expect those RSVPs to come back quickly.

Many websites have design templates for invitations. They allow you to customize your invitation and make it your own. It can be a creative and fun project if you enjoy this kind of work. If you would rather someone else do this for you, ask a friend or family member to help you or purchase your invitations through a company that will help design them for you.

Below is information that you should include in every wedding invitation:

- The names of the couple
- The guest(s) names (names of the children as well if you wish for them to come)
- Add a + 1 if the guest is single
- Wedding Date & Time
- Detailed Wedding Venue Information
- Start time of the ceremony and start time of reception
- Addresses of each venue
- Include directions to the venues printed on a separate insert
- RSVP requirements - how you wish for them to reply - by RSVP card or email or phone
- Wedding Registry Info - can be a separate insert

- Insert Options - dress code, accommodation details, parking, directions

Helpful Tip - *The informative inserts you are placing inside your invitation should match the look and feel of the invitation card. Have match-able moments every chance you get.*

6

Chapter 6 - Dress to Impress

I have seen many wedding guests not wear appropriate attire to a wedding. I've often wondered why someone would attend a wedding not dressed appropriately. If you are having a small casual wedding, there could be a logical explanation of why a guest would look like they just came back from an amusement park. But I would advise making it a goal to have your guests dressed to impress. After all, you two will look amazing for your wedding, so why shouldn't everyone else look their best too.

I once had a couple who had a beach wedding. The couple's wedding website and invitation reminded guests to wear appropriate footwear for the beach. The couple also reminded the guests that it could be hot that day. They gave examples and described the styles of clothing recommended for the wedding, such as knee-length or longer summer dresses for the ladies, lightweight button-down collared shirts and khakis, or neat Bermuda length shorts for the men. Did everyone dress this way for the wedding? Almost all of them did dress this way. The couple had great wedding photos because they effectively communicated the dress code for the wedding.

Here are some common phrases used on invitations to describe the style of attire you wish your guests to be wearing at your wedding:

- Casual Dress
- Semi-Formal Dress
- Cocktail Attire
- Smart Casual
- Formal or Black-Tie Optional
- Evening Chic
- Dressy Casual
- Casual Chic
- Fiesta Fashion
- Glitzy & Glamorous

Helpful Tip - You can come up with your dress catchphrase for communicating the style of attire to your guests, but please follow up with a description of that clothing. Your guests may not know or understand what "Evening Chic" means.

Themed weddings can sometimes break all the fashion rules. I once had a small wedding with a "Star Trek" theme. All 30 guests dressed up as a Star Trek character or alien. It was memorable and fun. Everyone was more than happy to be in costume and take pictures.

Many brides have told me they have always dreamed of their wedding and the white wedding gown they would wear. Even small weddings can make any person feel like a princess. What you have budgeted for your wedding dress or suit may be small. Wedding gowns, dresses, suits, and tuxedos are for rent at shops or online if your budget does not allow you to purchase them. Many of my savvy wedding couples have purchased their off-the-rack dress or suit at a department store.

Wedding dresses can also be re-purposed after your wedding. I had a friend who dyed her white wedding dress red after the wedding. She still wears this dress for formal events. I also have had clients wear a dress shirt and matching vest without a jacket. A jacket can be pricey. If the weather is warm, a nice dress shirt like a guayabera may be better than a traditional shirt and tie. A dressy shirt with matching trousers and dress shoes is a logical choice for a more casual type of wedding.

Some wear dresses, some wear suits, some wear costumes, and some wear absolutely nothing. I'll save the nude wedding story for a different time.

Whatever you decide to wear should complement what your partner is wearing and flow nicely with the theme of your wedding. A few years ago, I attended a wedding on an estate in a large house built to look like a castle. It was a formal-themed wedding, and all guests dressed in formal attire. The wedding theme was "Cinderella." The bride wore a beautiful blue gown as her wedding dress. Prince Charming wore a white tuxedo suit. At the start of the wedding reception, the couple made their grand entrance as a newlywed couple, and what they both wore to compliment their look was beautiful crowns on their heads. They looked like royalty.

7

Chapter 7 - Food & Beverage

Creating or selecting a food and beverage menu for your wedding can be easy work as long as you stay within your budget, know who your guests are, and know how much time you have allocated for the reception. What you choose to serve during your wedding can be decided by the time of day you are having the wedding. If you have the wedding reception venue rented for only 2-3 hours during the day, a brunch buffet or plated lunch may be the better choice. If you only have a couple of hours and it is a stand-up cocktail reception, then hors d'oeuvres will be the best option. If you have more time for your wedding, a more traditional or formal plated meal is an option. Communicating with a wedding/event coordinator, chef, or restaurant manager is crucial as they will guide you in selecting the best menu items while staying within your budget and time frame.

With a small wedding should you choose to have the reception at a restaurant, please remember to reserve the tables or space ahead of time. If you plan to have more than 15 people for a sit-down lunch or dinner, the restaurant may advise that they serve a pre-set or prix-fixe menu for your event and will assist you in pre-selecting menu options for your guests a week or more before your wedding day. A pre-selected menu for your event helps the staff execute service quickly so that you and your hungry guests will not have to wait too long for your food. Can you imagine 20 people all ordering 20 different entrees at the same time? Any restaurant kitchen would find it challenging to deliver the food promptly to your hungry guests, especially on a busy Saturday evening with other guests in the restaurant.

Most reception venues or caterers will charge a per person price for their food, whether you want a plated meal, hors d'oeuvres, or both at your wedding. Hors d'oeuvres can be served cold or hot, presented in chafing pans or trays on a table, or served on a tray and passed throughout the reception room by a server. In my years of pricing out menus for clients, hors d'oeuvres menus have always cost more per person than a pre-fixed plated meal menu. Caterers and other venues can also charge by the platter. Ask how many servings each platter has. If a platter of 8 miniature crab cakes serves only four people (two crabcakes per person), then with a group of 20 people, you know that you will need more than 4 or 5 platters. Also, depending on your budget, you may find that choosing the Chicken Satay Skewers would be a better value than the mini-crab cakes.

It also helps to know if anyone in your party has any food allergies. An allergic reaction to a guest can potentially ruin the happy mood for everyone. I once had a bride who was highly allergic to strawberries. The restaurant did its best to make there were no strawberries in any of the food at the wedding. However, one of the wedding guests ordered a Strawberry Daiquiri. The guest who drank the Strawberry Daiquiri kissed the bride on the cheek. Minutes later, the bride had a swollen cheek and broke out in hives. It was a bit of a scare for everyone, but she was a well-prepared bride and saved herself with the EpiPen she brought. She and all her guests enjoyed the rest of the evening versus a trip to the emergency room.

Drinks and Bar Packages - Many wedding venues offer different levels of drink or bar packages to choose from for your wedding. Here is a list of popular options that may be available to you. It is good to know what is included in each bar package as each venue may have different variations in their bar or drink packages.

Non-Alcoholic Drink Package - usually includes a selection of sodas, juices, iced teas, hot teas, and coffees. Some places include smoothies, non-alcoholic beer, and virgin cocktails.

Beer, Wine, and Soda Bar - usually includes bottled beers or beer on tap, House selected wines by the glass, selected sodas, and juice

Standard Bar - usually includes all drinks listed in a beer, wine, and soda bar package. Well liquors, select Call liquors, and pre-selected mixed cocktails may also be included.

Premium Bar - usually includes all of the above as well as selected premium top-shelf liquor

Consumption Open Bar - This bar package usually includes everything and is available to guests for a specific time during the reception. The client must approve the time frame for serving drinks, a time for last-call, and the time to close the bar. The client can also dictate the types of drinks that guests can order. Expect an added gratuity of 18-20% on the bill and pay the tab at the end of the event.

If you are planning a DIY wedding and creating your bar by purchasing your beverages at a package store, I would advise that you create a streamlined beverage menu for your reception. A limited drink menu makes it simpler for your guests to choose what they want to drink. You'll also save money too. Here is a list of beverages to purchase for your bar:

- Non-Alcoholic beverages - cola, diet cola, lemon-lime soda, ginger ale, club soda, tonic water, bottled water (still)
- Juice & Milk - Orange Juice, Cranberry Juice, and Milk
- White Wine - Chardonnay and Pinot Grigio
- Red Wine - Cabernet Sauvignon and Merlot
- Champagne or Sparkling Wine
- Liquors - Bourbon, Vodka, Gin, Rum, Scotch, and Tequila

Helpful Tip - Offer a signature cocktail for your wedding. Make sure it is an easy drink to make and an easy beverage to drink. (No flaming drinks please.)

Helpful Tip #2 - If you believe your bartender and waitstaff have given excellent service, be kind and tip them extra on top of the added gratuities on the bill. Weddings require much preparation. The staff at your wedding may have worked long hours preparing for your reception and should be rewarded for their efforts as long as they have provided excellent service.

8

Chapter 8 - The Crew

S mall weddings usually deal with fewer people helping you execute your big day. However, there will be a few vendors that you may have to hire to help make your wedding a success. Here is a list of people you may or may not need for your small wedding:

Wedding Planner - A wedding planner helps you plan your wedding. They usually charge by the hour. Many Wedding Planners work at wedding venues. Ask them how they will assist you with your wedding and what you should expect from them.

Independent Wedding Planners own their businesses and partner with specific wedding vendors. They have relationships with wedding vendors throughout the area which is helpful when planning your wedding. Be sure to schedule your time with wedding planners weeks or days in advance as they usually have many wedding clients getting married around the same time. A wedding planner can help you plan as little or as much as you want. They can handle all your invitations, accompany you to dress and suit fittings, help you choose floral and linen, etc. If you are having a small wedding, you may not need or want to pay for a wedding planner. However, if you do not have the time to plan your wedding, I highly advise having one.

Wedding Coordinator - If you are not hiring and utilizing a wedding planner to help you plan and execute your wedding, it may still be helpful to have a "Day of Wedding Coordinator." Most ceremony venues will provide one as part of their service. If they don't, I advise hiring an experienced wedding coordinator for the day. In this situation, it is best NOT to ask a friend or family member to coordinate your wedding unless that person is already an experienced wedding coordinator. A well-experienced wedding coordinator will assist and guide you through your wedding event. A good wedding coordinator will create a wedding itinerary and timeline for you to review and approve before your wedding day so that you will know what to expect that day. They will be there to cue the DJ or musicians when you walk down the aisle. They will help fix the train of your dress or assist the wedding photographer. They can even help guide your guests by getting them to their seats or another room. Believe me when I tell you that there have been many instances where wedding coordinators have prevented disasters from happening at weddings. A good wedding coordinator is worth every cent you spend.

Helpful Tip - *References, reviews, and an interview are must-haves when choosing and hiring a wedding planner or wedding coordinator.*

Florist - Compare prices with various florists for your floral needs. Keep in mind prices can vary from shop to shop but a floral shop may price match a competitor. Most florists deliver flowers 2-3 hours before the ceremony or reception. Communicate what time your events are and what time you expect to see the floral decor ready and in place on your wedding day. Many small weddings only utilize a small number of floral bouquets and arrangements. For these small weddings, you may want to look at floral warehouses in your area. Floral arrangements and bouquets can be ordered at wholesale prices in these large warehouses but know that you may have to arrange the flowers yourself.

Helpful Tip- Check out the florist shop's social media and website to see examples of their work from previous weddings.

Wedding Photographer - It's worth the money to hire a good photographer. A good photographer will offer clients different photo packages. Some may include engagement photos. Some may charge by the hour or by the number of photos they will take. I love a good photographer who edits photos well. Check out the photographer's website to see pictures before hiring them as your wedding photographer.

Bakery - I have always said a great wedding cake has the power to make the entire wedding great. If the wedding cake is dry and crumbly, every guest will remember that slice of cake. If your wedding cake looks incredible and tastes delicious, you will know because there will be many pictures taken of that wedding cake and guests asking you where you ordered the cake. Schedule cake tasting appointments with bakeries that specialize in wedding cakes. Have a picture prepared to show them what you wish your wedding cake to look like so that the baker can tell you if they can make your cake look like the one in your picture. Another option is to have a small cake for you and your spouse to cut with cupcakes for your guests. Wedding guests love cupcakes because they can easily take one home if they want to save it for later.

Waitstaff and Bartender(s) - Please tip your waitstaff and bar staff. Gratuity may be included in the price you have paid for food and beverage but keep in mind that service staff still only earn a little over minimum wage with tips. Be kind to the people who are working at your wedding. If, for any reason, you or your guests are not receiving the type of service you expect, communicate this with the Manager on Duty and your Wedding Coordinator immediately. Don't make a scene. That only makes everything worse for everyone.

DJ or Musicians/Band - If you have hired a DJ or a Band for your wedding, they may ask you to provide a list of your favorite songs so they can add a few of your favorites to their set list. It is also wise to ask them for their set list so that you can select which songs you want or don't want to play at your wedding. Before your wedding day, you should share the timeline and itinerary of events with the DJ or band. Also, how many sets would you like them to play? How long are the dance sets? How long will their breaks be (if any)? What types of dances will you have at your wedding? (Mother and Son Dance, the Money Dance, line dances, etc.) Will the band or DJ be able to eat wedding food on their break? Will you allow the DJ or band to drink alcoholic beverages or any beverages on your bill? Discuss these things with your entertainment folks before the wedding day. If you are uncomfortable asking these questions, ask someone to negotiate these concerns on your behalf or ask your wedding planner to manage this.

Hair & Make-Up - Hiring a Hair Stylist and Make-Up Artist (MUA) for your wedding is sometimes optional for a small wedding. You may be someone who feels like they can do their hair and make-up better than anyone else can. If this is you, then there is no need to hire an expert to do this for you. Want to feel spoiled? Want to look your best on your wedding day? Hire an M.U.A and hairstylist. They will be worth it to help you look and feel like a million bucks for your big day.

Transportation, Lighting, Linen, Dance floor, Tent, Tables, and more - These wedding extras are usually for the larger wedding. If you are a small wedding and believe you require these items, I would ask your wedding planner for help and guidance as they will know who the best vendors are. They may even find a solution that allows you to have the wedding without them.

Helpful Tip - *Read any rental agreements, service agreements, or contracts carefully before signing them with a vendor. Ensure the date and times on the order are correct. Read and understand the cancellation policies. If you cancel your wedding for any reason, the services or items from the vendor are subject to a cancellation fee of up to 100% of the cost.*

9

Chapter 9 - The Day Before

The day before the wedding will be busy. Regardless of how busy you are, calling your vendors is an important task that should be completed earlier in the day. I would not recommend asking a friend or family member to do this for you.

There once was a Maid of Honor who was a close friend of the couple getting married. The couple asked for her help and asked her to call the bakery to confirm the drop-off time for their wedding cake. She forgot to call. The cake was delivered too early in the morning. It sat on a cake table in front of a window all day. The cake melted and drooped because it was a warm and sunny day. If the bakery had delivered the cake an hour before the reception began, the cake would have survived.

Your friends and family at your wedding will be just as excited as you the day before your wedding. Try to refrain from asking them for their help with anything important this day. If they offer to help, kindly thank them but say, "No, Thank You." Important "day before the wedding" tasks should be done by you.

Wedding To-Do List for the day before the Wedding:

- **Call and Check in with your Wedding Coordinator, Venue, and Vendors.** If you have a wedding coordinator assisting you, then they can call your vendors for you to confirm arrival or delivery times. If you do not have a wedding coordinator, I advise you to call and speak with each vendor personally. Also, if you are paying any vendors the final payment at the wedding, ensure the checks are ready and ask your wedding coordinator, family member, or close friend to give those checks to the vendors that require payment.
- **Wedding timeline and itinerary** – Everyone working your wedding (including vendors) should have a copy of your finalized timeline and itinerary. Review this with your wedding coordinator if you have one working with you.
- **Pack your Stuff.** Pack your wedding clothes, accessories, undergarments, shoes, a change of clothes, make-up, hairspray, jewelry, etc. Don't forget to pack up any gifts you may be giving out to loved ones or decor that you have made for the wedding. Remember to bring all your tech and make sure all batteries for that tech are charged up at 100% before leaving. This means any cell phones, tablets, cameras, drones, lighting, cordless microphone, tripods, cords, speakers, etc. Don't forget to bring your purse with your wallet and checkbook and any paperwork that needs to be signed. Bring a copy of your vows, the wedding rings, and a handkerchief or tissues for you or anyone near you who needs it. And items that I always advise brides to bring that may not be on their list are an emergency sewing kit, breath mints, lotion, a nice jacket or blazer in case they get cold, and 2 pairs of shoes. A pair to wear during the reception such as comfortable dress flats and a pair to wear after the reception such as sneakers.
- **Rings** – Rings can be given to the Best Man or ring bearer to hold but I would advise waiting until right before the ceremony before giving the rings to them. Just remember to pack them and take

them with you.

- **Stay hydrated by drinking plenty of water.** Drinking plenty of water will make your skin look incredible the next day and ready for all the picture-taking. You will also have more energy if you are well hydrated. It's best to avoid drinking alcohol the day before your wedding to prevent looking puffy and swollen.

- **Eat healthy food** and stay away from foods high in salt or foods that may have the potential to make you sick. Think low-fat, high protein, with nutritious fruits and vegetables. Eating these foods help your body stay energized through the long and busy day ahead. Don't try to fast on the day before your wedding. You could faint or be sick on your wedding day if you haven't eaten properly the day before.

- **Practice your Vows and any other speeches you will be giving.** Make sure you have written them down on paper and have them close by in case you forget what to say. It's okay to read your vows written on a notecard. It is better to read them than to forget what to say and blunder it all.

- **Write a letter.** Today is a perfect day to write a letter to the love of your life. Take a moment to write how you feel about getting married and how you feel right now. This letter is for your future spouse to read before the ceremony.

- **Get a good night's sleep**. Wind down for bed early this night and do things that help you relax. Read a book, have your feet rubbed, watch a movie, meditate, etc. Stay away from any person who might cause you stress. What you want to avoid is having a bunch of people around you. Limit yourself to being with only one or two best friends that evening.

10

Chapter 10 - The Wedding Day

Today is the big day! Here are a few tips to make sure your day goes well.

- Ask your MOH (Maid of Honor) and BM (Best Man) to help make sure every person is in place and not wandering around before the ceremony begins. If your small wedding only has a MOH and BM, that's perfect. No need to worry about getting every person in place. You also have the assistance of your wedding coordinator.
  - If you have a big wedding dress or a long train wedding gown, ask your MOH to help you with it during the wedding and to bustle you at the start of your reception.
  - Eat your food! You paid for it! I often see couples who do not eat and spend the entire wedding visiting with their friends and family. Share your first meal as a newlywed couple and eat together while your friends and family eat.
  - Limit your intake of alcohol. A few years ago, a bride drank multiple shots of liquor before the ceremony. She also had glasses of wine right after the ceremony. She then drank champagne during the entire wedding reception.

By the end of the evening, she was drunk. She was so intoxicated that she lifted her skirt to show everyone what she was wearing underneath her dress. It was not a pretty sight. Her newlywed husband was not happy. Celebrating with a glass or two of wine or champagne is fine, but don't get drunk. It's not attractive.

- If you plan on having your DJ or band play a song for your Dad & Daughter dance or Mother and Son dance, play only a portion of the song or invite others to join in and dance after a minute or so. A song could last 3 minutes or more. Most people start to lose interest after a minute of watching two people dance. Unless you have some exciting choreography happening, keep those songs short.

- There are different laws in each state. Be sure you have signed the wedding certificate and that it is processed. Your wedding officiant should know what to do and will advise you on what needs to be done with any wedding documents to ensure your marriage is legal.

- Don't ever go barefoot. Your feet may hurt in those heels. The same may go for the women wearing heels at your wedding. However, they should not remove their shoes. Most venues have a policy that guests must have shoes on at all times. This rule is in place for your protection in case there is any broken glass on the floor. Change into the comfy flats or sneakers you brought and let others know they too can change into their extra pair of shoes.

- Don't run out of food or drinks. If the food starts to run out and your guests are still hungry, ask the manager for more food to be served and purchase more food. If they can't prepare more food for your wedding, ask them to start the dessert service or the wedding cake. If you are having a DIY wedding, send someone to a store or restaurant to purchase more food or plan on ending your event sooner rather than later.

- Have Fun! We can always aim for a perfect wedding, but the truth is something will not go the way you expect. That's okay. Having a relaxed attitude can help with any stressful moments that might arise. The trick is to not let anything or anyone ruin your mood on this special day. If something goes wrong, know that it may not seem funny to you at this time. But, whatever happens, it will be a great story to remember and tell in the future.

11

Resources

17 TIPS ON HOW TO PICK A WEDDING VENUE. (2020, February 28). Minted.Com. Retrieved July 20, 2022, from https://www.minted.com/wedding-ideas/wedding-venue-tips

These Are the Best Websites for Designing Wedding Invitations. (2022, June 23). Brides.Com. Retrieved July 20, 2022, from https://www.brides.com/story/best-websites-for-wedding-invitations

Wedding Dress Code 101. (n.d.). Invitationsbydawn.Com. Retrieved July 20, 2022, from https://www.invitationsbydawn.com/content/wedding-dress-code-101/

From Casual to Dazzle. (2003, November). Oprah.Com. Retrieved July 20, 2022, from https://www.oprah.com/style/from-casual-to-dazzle-our-dress-code-glossary/all

Wedding Countdown: What To Do The Night Before Your Wedding. (n.d.).

Kennedyblue.Com. Retrieved July 20, 2022, from https://www.kenn edyblue.com/blogs/weddings/36240516-wedding-countdown-what-to-do-the-night-before-your-wedding

12

Conclusion

I hope this book has shared enough information that you now feel a bit more prepared and confident that your small wedding will be exactly the way you want it. Thank you for taking the time to read this book. More event planning books are planned for the future as part of this series and I look forward to sharing them with you. I wish you a wonderful and memorable wedding! ~ j.f.f

If you have found this book helpful, please be kind enough to leave a favorable review on Amazon. Thank You!

Made in United States
North Haven, CT
06 March 2023

33673093R00024